YOU CHOOSE

CAN YOU SURVIVE
the Great San Francisco
EARTHQUAKE?

AN INTERACTIVE HISTORY ADVENTURE

by Ailynn Collins

CAPSTONE PRESS
a capstone imprint

Published by Capstone Press, a Capstone imprint.
1710 Roe Crest Drive
North Mankato, Minnesota 56003
capstonepub.com

Copyright © 2022 by Capstone. All rights reserved. No part of this publication may be reproduced in whole or in part, or stored in a retrieval system, or transmitted in any form or by any means, electronic, mechanical, photocopying, recording, or otherwise, without written permission of the publisher.

Library of Congress Cataloging-in-Publication Data is available
on the Library of Congress website.
ISBN 9781663958945 (library binding)
ISBN 9781666323573 (paperback)
ISBN 9781666323580 (eBook PDF)

Summary: On April 18, 1906, a huge earthquake rocks and shakes the city of San Francisco, California. Even worse, the quake causes huge fires to break out across the city. Can you escape your damaged home before it collapses? Will you help the firefighters try to save the city from the devastating fires? Will you be accused of looting while helping someone escape the rubble? It's up to YOU to survive one of the worst earthquakes ever recorded.

Editorial Credits
Editor: Aaron Sautter; Designer: Bobbie Nuytten; Media Researcher: Morgan Walters; Production Specialist: Laura Manthe

All internet sites appearing in back matter were available and accurate when this book was sent to press.

Printed and bound in China. 5370

TABLE OF CONTENTS

About Your Adventure.....................5

CHAPTER 1
The End of the World?......................7

CHAPTER 2
Escaping A Nightmare.....................11

CHAPTER 3
Battling the Blaze........................49

CHAPTER 4
Chinatown Disaster.......................81

CHAPTER 5
Aftermath................................103

    More About Earthquakes..................106
    Other Paths to Explore..................108
    Bibliography............................109
    Glossary................................110
    Read More...............................111
    Internet Sites..........................112
    About the Author........................112

ABOUT YOUR ADVENTURE

It's 1906, and you're living in the beautiful city of San Francisco, California. The weather is pleasant, and your family likes going to Golden Gate Park. You also enjoy the city's famous hills and trolley cars.

But on April 18, the city is rocked by a terrible earthquake. Hundreds of buildings are destroyed. Fires quickly spread across the city. Will you survive through the massive destruction?

Chapter One sets the scene. Then you choose which path to read. Follow the directions at the bottom of the page as you read the stories. The decisions you make will change your outcome. After you finish one path, go back and read the others for new perspectives and more adventures.

Turn the page to begin your adventure.

When it opened in 1875, the Palace Hotel became one of the grandest features of downtown San Francisco.

CHAPTER 1
THE END OF THE WORLD?

San Francisco in the early 1900s was known as the "Paris of America." It was famous for its culture and industry. The city was the ninth largest in the United States and the most important city on the west coast.

Everything in San Francisco was big—from the Palace Hotel to City Hall. Its largest department store was called the Emporium. San Francisco's Chinatown area was the most crowded of any outside of Asia. The United States Mint, where gold was kept and money was printed, had one-third of the country's gold supplies.

Turn the page.

By 1906, more than 400,000 people lived in San Francisco. They thought of their city as the most beautiful in the world. It had a lively theater and opera scene. The Grand Opera House could hold more than 2,800 people.

The night of April 17, 1906, is a typical cool and clear San Francisco evening. Opera fans are wowed by a magical performance by famous singer Enrico Caruso. Afterward, some go for a walk to enjoy the lovely evening.

From the top of Telegraph Hill, a person can see most of the beautifully lit city. As each person goes to bed, nobody imagines that their happy lives will soon be interrupted by something terrible.

Before the sun rises on April 18, the city is shaken violently. People sleeping peacefully are violently thrown from their beds and knocked against walls. Buildings collapse across the city, spilling broken bricks, glass, and wood into the streets. The roads split open, and thick smoke fills the air. Hundreds of people are hurt, or worse.

During the night you had great dreams, but now you're living in a nightmare. You're lucky to be alive. For now, at least. But your ordeal is just beginning. Will you make it to the end of the day?

To be a young boy and escape your shaking house, turn to page 11.

To be a firefighter and try to save the city, turn to page 49.

To be a single mother trying to save your business, turn to page 81.

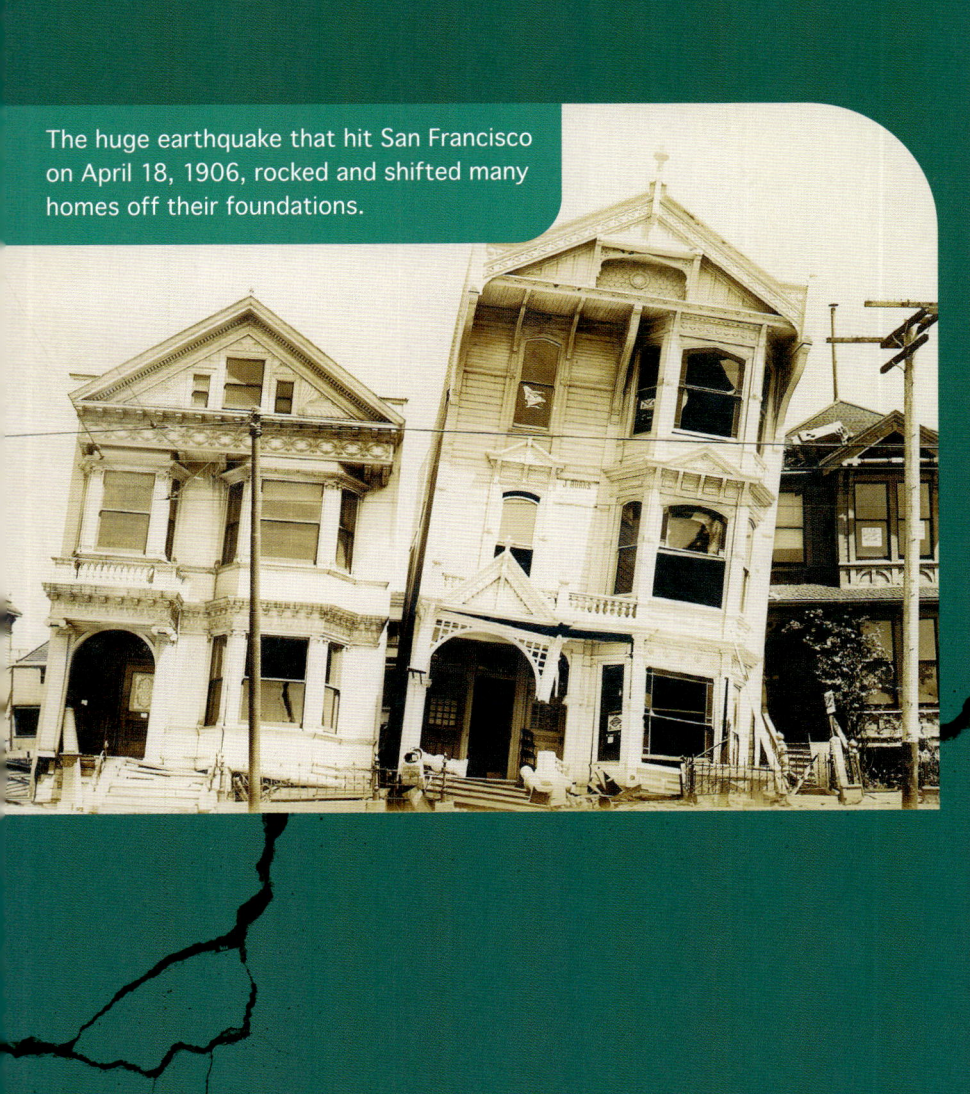

The huge earthquake that hit San Francisco on April 18, 1906, rocked and shifted many homes off their foundations.

CHAPTER 2
ESCAPING A NIGHTMARE

You're half asleep when you hear screaming from the next room. You open your eyes and feel yourself being tossed like a salad in your own bed.

"What's happening?" you cry, but no one answers.

The sound of glass breaking sends chills up your spine. Your father is shouting something, but the rumbling from the shaking house drowns out his words. Your heart is racing. As you hang on to the bedposts, you struggle to think clearly. You're only 11 years old, and you've never been this scared.

To hide in bed under your covers, turn to page 12.

To do what you think Father would do, turn to page 13.

You don't dare to leave the bed. Glass shatters around you. A piece of the ceiling crashes down onto your bed, missing your head by inches.

Now you're shaking too—with fear. All you can do is pull the covers over you as the room shakes. Suddenly, the bed slides to the other end of the room and crashes into a wall. The window explodes, spraying glass all over you.

You can hear Mother screaming, and Father is still shouting. Will they come to rescue you? You fall to your left and then get jerked to your right. You hold on to your mattress for dear life.

BOOM! Something sounds like it explodes in the room. The last thing you remember is the pain of something heavy crashing onto you. You are one of the first victims of this terrible earthquake.

THE END

To follow another path, turn to page 9.
To learn more about the earthquake, turn to page 103.

You spot a pair of shoes sliding around your room. You grab them and quickly slip them on. You run out the bedroom door and duck just as a piece of the ceiling collapses to the floor behind you.

You dash down the stairs to find your parents. The house rolls like ocean waves. Cracks in the stairs appear as you jump over several steps. You cross the living room and duck into the kitchen just as the paintings on the hallway wall come crashing down. As quickly as it started, the shaking stops.

"Is it over?" you call out.

"Not likely," Father says. He appears in the room, carrying a large stuffed bag. "There's more to come, I'm sure of it."

Mother grabs as much food as she can. Maisy, your little sister, watches from her playpen.

"Get Maisy to the backyard, John," Mother says. "Father and I will follow as soon as we can."

Turn the page.

You pick up Maisy and rush outside. You step carefully through broken dishes that have fallen out of the china cabinet.

You make it to the yard just as the next tremor hits. You huddle in the corner farthest away from the house. This tremor is even stronger than the first and lasts a lot longer. The lawn rolls like the house did earlier. It's followed by a loud cracking sound as the ground splits open in front of you. You scream and push hard against the fence.

When the quaking ends, you finally breathe a sigh of relief. You can't believe the size of the long crack in the yard. Maisy is sobbing.

"We're all right!" Mother calls. She and Father step outside with more bundles. You run to help them, careful to avoid the crack in the ground.

Father has the old camping tent. Mother has blankets, shoes, and food.

The powerful earthquake opened huge cracks in city streets and people's yards.

"We may have to live in the yard for a few days," Father says. "It'll be like camping in the woods." He's trying to sound cheerful as he sets up the tent. But you can tell he's as scared as you are.

Inside the tent, you hang on to each other as several small tremors shake the ground beneath you. At least the ground isn't splitting open anymore.

Turn the page.

Over the yard fence, people are screaming and crying. You also hear the sound of wheels rumbling over the road, and in the distance, you hear an explosion.

"What was that?" you ask.

"Probably a gas line blowing up," Father says.

"That means there'll be fire," Mother adds. She sounds worried.

When all grows silent, Father announces that the earthquake is over. You leave the tent. The air smells as if everything in the area is burning.

"I'm going to inspect the house," Father says.

To stay outside with your mother and sister, go to page 17.

To to with your father, turn to page 21.

"The damage doesn't seem too bad," Father says when he returns.

You all follow him back inside. Other than some broken windows and a few cracks, your house withstood the worst of the earthquake. You help Father bring out more food, an old camp stove, and whatever utensils you can find. There's a precious jug of water that's still undamaged. You're careful not to spill it as you carry it to the tent.

Father heads out the front door. When he reappears, he's accompanied by two neighbor families.

"They've lost their homes," Father explains. "I've invited them to share what little we have."

Soon there are five families sharing your yard. They've brought what little they could salvage, and everyone shares. You walk around and hand out the sandwiches Mother has made.

Turn the page.

It's strangely quiet in the backyard, even though you count at least 25 people here. No one speaks much. They just stare up at the sky or down at their few belongings. No one cries, screams, or chatters. Everyone is in shock.

"Why don't we cook something on our stove?" Mother suggests at last.

This idea cheers people up. Father starts a fire in a corner of the yard. People stand around the fire, warming their hands, while Mother prepares to cook a soup.

KABOOM! Another explosion, this one much closer, rocks the neighborhood. If there are gas leaks nearby, maybe it's not safe to have a fire going.

To continue warming up around the fire, go to page 19.
To put out the fire, turn to page 20.

Even though the sun has fully risen, you feel cold. The warmth of the fire feels too good to put it out. Together with the neighbors, you stand around the campfire in the yard. No one talks about the explosions. Everyone acts as if they're safe right here. You inhale the wonderful smell of Mother's soup.

BOOM! You hear another explosion. It came from inside your house! Flames blow through the back door and into your small yard. It joins with the campfire you're standing next to.

No one has time to react. Sadly, you, your family, and your neighbors all die in the fire.

THE END

To follow another path, turn to page 9.
To learn more about the earthquake, turn to page 103.

"If the gas lines are exploding, is it safe to have a fire out here?" you ask Father.

Just then, a young fireman appears at the gate. He calls Father over. They have a long talk. Then Father returns and puts out the fire.

"The firemen are having a hard time containing the big fires," he says. "They don't want any new ones to start."

"What are we to do then?" Mother asks.

Father sighs. "The authorities have asked this entire neighborhood to evacuate. If they can't contain the fires, we're all in danger. There's a refugee camp in Golden Gate Park. We'll have to head there."

With barely a word of protest, the people gather up their belongings and move out.

Turn to page 22.

You and Father cautiously enter the house.

CRACK! A floorboard cracks loudly and splits under your feet. Father catches you before you fall into the hole. Then a plank from the ceiling crashes down into the kitchen.

"Run!" Father calls, and you both dash out the door.

"We should leave the property," Father says once you're safely back outside. He peers over the fence. "People seem to be heading in one direction. We'll just follow them."

You help Father pull down the tent and load everything onto two small wagons. With a heavy heart, you leave your house. When you went to bed last night, you never imagined you'd lose your home in a matter of hours.

Turn the page.

The earthquake caused fires that spread to hundreds of buildings across the city.

You pull Maisy along in a wagon. You take one last look at your house as you cross the street and head north.

At the end of the block, you stop in horror. Smoke billows out of several houses. In one house, flames leap out of the rooftop and into the air.

"We must hurry," Father calls out.

He leads your family up to Market Street, where many fancy buildings are found. There's a famous hotel there. It's still standing, though everything on either side of the hotel now lies in ruin. You see people digging through the rubble, trying to get to those trapped beneath.

As you continue, you're blinded by dust, and the street is thick with debris. You dodge pieces of wood that threaten to trip you up everywhere. Occasionally, water flows across your path.

"The water mains must have burst," Father says.

"Don't look!" Mother cries, as you pass a house that's on fire. But you can't help it, and you turn to look.

A woman is running with her coat on fire. Father rushes to her and pulls her to the ground. He makes her roll over until the fire is out. Then he lifts her to her feet.

Turn the page.

"Thank you so much, sir," she gasps, trembling. "My name is Mary Lee, and I was just cleaning that home. It's all gone now. Luckily, the family is away on vacation."

Mother gives her half of a leftover sandwich. Mary gobbles it greedily. Then she heads to Chinatown to check on her own family.

As you turn to continue on your way, you hear your parents gasp, "Oh no!" They're looking at a badly damaged hospital on the corner. Firemen and others are carrying the sick away.

"Keep moving," Father says urgently. "We must get to safety."

You walk quickly along Market Street. The air smells bad. It chokes you with each breath. You and Maisy cover your faces with scarves.

People stream out from every street corner. They haul strange items like sewing machines and bird cages. One woman even pushes a baby carriage loaded with fur coats.

"When people panic, you never know what they will consider to be precious," Mother says.

You notice something. "People are heading in two directions."

Father stops to ask a policeman where everyone is going.

"Some people are headed to the Ferry Building," the policeman replies. "You could go with them and try to get on a ferry away from the city. Or you may want to follow the others to Golden Gate Park. A relief camp is being set up there."

To go to Golden Gate Park, turn to page 26.
To head to the Ferry Building, turn to page 44.

"We should head to the park," your parents decide.

"Be careful where you step," Mother says, as you look down the street. The sidewalks are cracked and broken. Some look like they've been flipped upside down. Electric cables dangle about dangerously, sparking small flames. On some side streets, water flows everywhere.

"How will the firemen put out the fires when the water is leaking out like that?" you ask.

"It certainly won't be easy," Father sighs. You dodge firemen and their horse-drawn engines as they trot gingerly past.

You join a crowd and walk in silence for what seems like hours until you reach Golden Gate Park. The park is full of people who've lost their homes. Groups huddle together around small fires.

After the earthquake hit, a refugee camp was set up at Fort Mason in Golden Gate Park.

Tents have been set up in neat rows. Father finds a tent for your family, and you all pile inside and fall asleep immediately.

The next day, you look out over the city from the top of a hill. You can see everything from where you are.

"Oh, my," Father exclaims. "The city is on fire!"

Turn the page.

You look on in horror. Smoke billows from every street. Buildings look like they have gaping holes in their sides. Most of them are charred, and nothing but a few beams are left sticking out of the ground. The heat from the fires can be felt all the way from where you stand. Occasionally, you hear the boom of an explosion.

In spite of the horrific scene before you, the park itself is quiet. People just go about their business. It is eerily silent.

The next day, your father wants to go back to the city to check on your house. Your mother insists you all stay and help give out food and water to the refugees.

"We need to stay active," Mother says. "We should volunteer to help."

To volunteer at the park, go to page 29.
To go with Father into the city, turn to page 33.

Before you can ask Mother what to do, she walks toward the middle of the park. There, people stand at stations handing out water to others waiting in long lines. Mother talks to the person in charge and volunteers you both. She's carrying Maisy in a bundle strapped to her back so her arms are free to work.

Homeless refugees had to wait in long lines to get supplies of food and water.

You spend the morning serving water to a line of people that doesn't seem to end. Still, they're all happy to see you.

When you get a break, you wander off to a small open field. Children about your age are playing ball. You join them, and for a little while, it feels as if life hasn't changed.

When a bell rings, it's time to line up for food. You help your mother serve meals. Donations have been flowing in all day from people in other places who heard about the disaster. When you're done, you're too tired to eat. You fall asleep in your tent and don't wake until the next morning.

The city below continues to burn. For the next few days, you help out where you can by serving people water and food. When you get free time, you take Maisy for walks and play in the open field.

The crowd grows smaller each day as people find ways to leave the city.

On Saturday you wake to rain. You feel hopeful. Father has finally returned and is speaking quietly with Mother. But you've never seen him look so sad and tired.

"The fires are finally out. But we've lost our house," he says. "Everything is gone."

"What are we going to do?" you ask. You can't imagine living in the park forever.

"We'll have to take a train out of the city," Father says.

Mother hugs you for a long time. "We have family in southern California. We'll move there for a while."

"We'll rebuild somehow," Father says, sniffing. "San Franciscans are hardy people. We'll come back, someday."

Turn the page.

That makes you feel a little better. Rain falls the rest of the day, helping to put out the remaining fires. Your family makes their way through the rain to the railway station. The trains are transporting refugees away from the city for free. As the train pulls away, you say a silent goodbye to the ruined city.

THE END

To follow another path, turn to page 9.
To learn more about the earthquake, turn to page 103.

"Stay close to me," Father tells you as you leave the park. You head back into the city, down to Market Street. You see posters have been put up everywhere. They all say the same thing. When you stop to read one of them, Father tries to shield you with his arm.

"Let's not linger about," he says.

"Father, this poster says the police will shoot us on sight if they think we're looting," you say. "What's looting?"

Father pulls you away, and you continue to walk. "Looting is when people take things from damaged stores. It's a form of stealing."

You and Father step around rubble from buildings that have collapsed into the street. You also hop over many smelly puddles of dark water. You think about his words as you run past a building that's on fire.

Turn the page.

Many people dug through the rubble looking for anything valuable they could steal.

Just then, a fire engine pulled by three terrified horses barrels down the street. You jump out of the way and watch the firefighters twist and turn by obstacles in the road. But the wagon is moving too fast. It suddenly tilts, and two of the firemen almost fall off.

Then, behind you, you hear a shot ring out. It makes you jump. Father grabs your hand and pulls you down a side street. You turn to see what's happened just as Father rounds the corner. A policeman, gun in hand, stands over the body of a man.

Was that man looting? you wonder. A shiver runs through your body, even though the heat from the fires is making everything feel really hot.

Before you can recover from the shock of seeing a dead body, you hear something.

"What's that, Father?" you ask, stopping in your tracks.

"What's what?" he says.

You make Father stop and listen. Among the chaos of blazing fires and people running away, you hear the faint sound of a cry.

Turn the page.

"Help! Help me, please!"

It's coming from a pile of rubble in front of you.

"There's someone trapped in there!" you shout.

"Someone will come by to help them," Father says. "We must get to our house before the fires destroy everything."

You want to do as Father says, but you hear the cry for help again.

>To help the trapped person, go to page 37.
>To keep heading toward home, turn to page 41.

Father hears the cry too. He hesitates, but then agrees that you can't leave someone trapped under the rubble. You climb up onto a pile of broken boards and bricks and listen again.

"Help!" The cry is clear but weak. It's coming from beneath you.

You and Father quickly begin moving pieces of wood and stone. Soon, two soldiers arrive to help. It takes several minutes before you can see a hole in the rubble.

You hear a woman coughing.

"Here!" you shout.

Together, you dig until you reach the woman's hand. You hold on to it as the men drag away more debris until she's free. You're amazed at how she survived. She's covered in dirt. Her legs are clearly broken, as they hang at an odd angle.

Turn the page.

"Thank you," she croaks, as the soldiers lay her carefully on the pavement.

"Run down the street to the fire engine and get them to send an ambulance," Father tells you. "We'll keep digging for more survivors."

You search the streets for the fire engine you saw earlier. It's sitting in front of the ruins of the grand Palace Hotel, the one you passed on your way to Golden Gate Park. But now the hotel is just a pile of smoking debris.

You run up to a fireman, who's just putting away a hose.

You tell him about the woman you've found. He listens with a grave expression.

"Good for you, son," he says. "But the hospital's been burned to the ground. The dead are being sent to our fire station as we speak. The survivors will have to go to Golden Gate Park."

"Could you call for an ambulance to come?" you ask.

He shakes his head. "All the telephone and telegraph lines are down. We can't even communicate with other fire stations. But the military has just come into the city. Maybe they'll be able to help. In the meantime, you should stay where you are with the survivors. Hopefully an ambulance will drive by."

That isn't much help. You run back to Father. The soldiers are loading the injured woman onto an old wagon pulled by a horse. You also see two other bodies laying on the ground nearby.

"Did you find more survivors?" you ask Father.

He gently turns you toward himself. "No, son. No one else is alive in there. I don't want you to look upon the dead. It's not something you will forget easily."

Turn the page.

After the earthquake, workers frantically dug through the rubble to search for survivors.

But you insist on looking. You're saddened to see a man about Father's age. He's covered in dust and looks like he's sleeping. The other is a young woman. You think about how their families must feel about losing them. You wipe away the tear that rolls down your face.

"Let's go, son," Father says after a moment. "We have to get to our house."

You and Father walk, run, and dodge the fires along the roads. Finally, you reach the street your house is on. You say a silent prayer for your home. Many of the houses you've just passed are burned to a crisp.

You breathe a deep sigh of relief when you see that the fires haven't reached your house. It's still standing.

"We must be careful," Father warns as you try to dash inside.

Slowly, you make it into the yard. There are traces of the belongings your family and neighbors left behind. You look up at the house and notice how it seems to be tilting. Several roof tiles have fallen off, and the steps leading up to the house are broken.

Father enters the house first. When he reappears, he motions for you to enter.

Turn the page.

"Gather as many things as you can from your room," he says. "Take only what you can carry—and be quick about it."

You go to your room and pull out the biggest bag you have. You stuff it with a few clothes and some books.

When you return to the yard, Father's clutching two bags in each hand and talking to a fireman. His shoulders are slumped.

As you're leaving the house, a loud boom shakes the ground under your feet. "Is that another quake?" you shriek.

"The fires are spreading to our neighborhood. To stop them, the firefighters will have to blow up our homes," Father says with a sigh. "We should be glad we were able to save some of our things."

He wipes a tear away. "The important thing is that we're all safe."

You both turn up the street, heading back to your family. "We'll return someday and rebuild. San Franciscans are a tough bunch. The city will return to its full glory again."

Another boom sends shocks through you. You don't understand how blowing up houses will stop fires, but you know Father isn't in the mood to talk about it now.

"We'll take the train to my brother's house in southern California," Father says. "When it's safe, we'll find a way to come home again."

You take one last look at the neighborhood—the only one you've ever known. With a heavy heart, you readjust the bag slung over your shoulder. You walk away, trying not to think of your home collapsing into rubble.

THE END

To follow another path, turn to page 9.
To learn more about the earthquake, turn to page 103.

"Let's head to the docks," Mother suggests. "We can try and get on a ferry to the other side of the bay."

"Be careful where you step," Father says, as he looks down the street. The sidewalks are cracked and broken. Chunks of concrete have been tossed about everywhere. Electrical cables swing about dangerously, sparking small flames. The air stinks of gas and sewage. The smoke from the fires doesn't help you breathe either. You cover Maisy's face with a scarf and tie one across your nose too.

"How will the firemen put out the fires when the water is pouring down the streets?" you ask.

"They have their work cut out for them," Father sighs. You dodge firemen and their horse-drawn engines as they trot gingerly up and down the street.

You follow the crowd that trudges in silence toward the sea. An explosion stops you in your tracks. Some people scream. You look to Father for help. He's staring at a building going up in flames.

"The gas lines are bursting everywhere!" he cries.

Your family picks up the pace until you reach the Ferry Building. You look up in alarm. A wall of the Ferry Building has fallen into the bay. The clock tower leans dangerously to one side. But it's still standing.

Fireboats in the bay pump salt water continuously to try to save oceanfront warehouses. Still, you can see fires in the distance, burning up the piers along the water. It's only a matter of time before the flames reach the Ferry Building.

Turn the page.

Someone yells for people to stand in line. "You'll all get a space on a ferry soon enough!" the man shouts. "Please, be patient."

Surprisingly, everyone obeys without complaint. The line snakes around the block. You and your family wait for what feels like forever. Once in a while a ferry arrives, and the line moves forward. But there are so many people. Will your family make it to safety before fires burn up the whole terminal?

Maisy falls asleep in her wagon. Your stomach growls. Mother goes off to find some food and returns with a small amount of fruit.

"They were giving away these oranges," she says. "The shop owners lost their stores, but they're happy to help their hungry neighbors." The fruit makes the waiting easier.

At last, it's your family's turn. You notice that private boats are being used along with the ferries. People have volunteered their own boats to help move others to safety. You pile onto a small wooden boat with several other refugees.

As the boat pulls away from the dock, you pass Navy ships arriving in the bay. They're here to help put out fires.

As the boat travels across the water, you look back at the city where you were born.

"We'll be back someday," Father says. "I'm sure people here will rebuild."

You sigh and say a silent farewell to San Francisco. You wonder how long it will be before you see your home city again.

THE END

To follow another path, turn to page 9.
To learn more about the earthquake, turn to page 103.

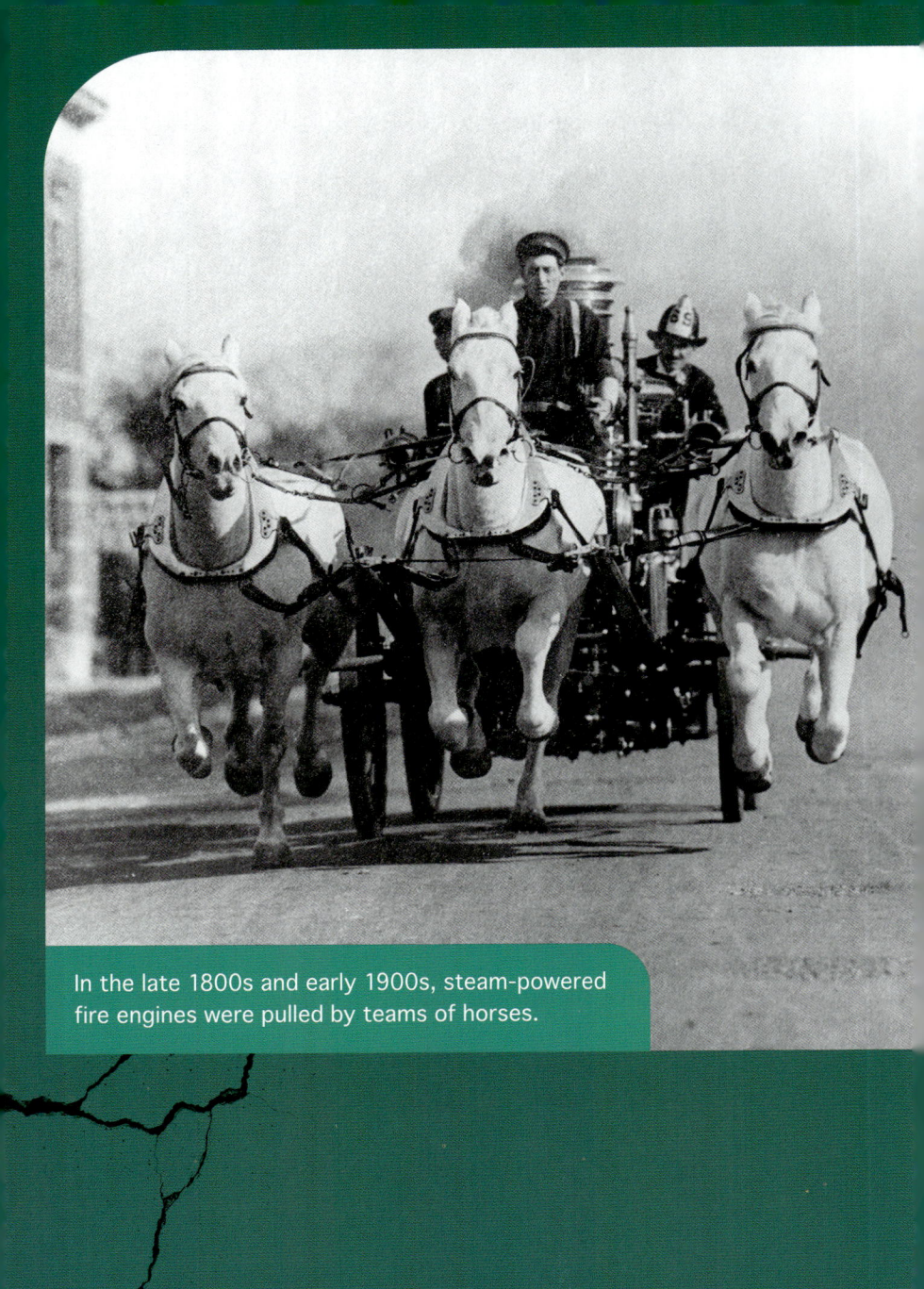

In the late 1800s and early 1900s, steam-powered fire engines were pulled by teams of horses.

CHAPTER 3
BATTLING THE BLAZE

It took a lot of training to finally become a firefighter. You love your job. You and your wife just had your first baby. And yesterday, you were promoted to squad leader. Life is going great.

But in the early morning hours of April 18, 1906, you wake up to a strange rumbling sound. As you sit up, the floor beneath you shakes violently. You're thrown out of bed and onto the floor.

Cries of shock spread throughout the fire station. You crawl under the bed and begin to count the seconds. You get to 40 and lose count. You've heard about earthquakes and have trained for them, but this is the first time you've experienced one.

Turn the page.

When the shaking stops, you quickly slip into your uniform.

"Why have the alarms not gone off?" you ask your fellow fireman.

"Nothing's working," he says, as you both run to the barn where the fire horses are. They're whinnying loudly in fear.

Suddenly, you feel a second tremor hit. The ground rolls like waves on the sea. You duck into the stables and stand at the doorway. The horses are panicking.

As soon as the quake ends, you calm the horses and hitch them to the fire and hose engines.

"We need to get them out of the barns before the buildings collapse!" you shout to your fellow firemen. Everyone in your station works to move the horses and engines out to safety. So far, your building seems to be stable.

"All communication systems are down," the station chief announces. "No telephones or telegraphs seem to be working. We have to get out there and see what needs to be done."

Fire and hose engines are divided into two teams. One team will head north to the hospital, and the other will head south.

"Do what you can, boys," the chief says. "And report back soon. Stay safe."

To head north to the hospital, turn to page 52.

To check out damage to the south, turn to page 59.

You drive the fire engine. It's pulled by three horses and carries four other firemen. The hose engine follows behind you. You guide the horses quickly but carefully through the dangerous streets. Debris from collapsed buildings is spread all over the roads. The streets themselves have deep gashes in them. Guiding the horses is hard, and they snort with fear.

To force the horses through their fear, go to page 53.

To retreat and try another route, turn to page 54.

It was almost impossible to guide the fire wagons through the city's broken and cracked streets.

You urge the horses to keep moving. In front of you, the street opens up like a giant mouth. A deep chasm appears. On the opposite side of the street, a building crumbles like a sand castle. A few beams are stopped by crates of fruit that lie on the street. You're so stunned as you watch the collapsing building that you don't notice when the horses run your engine right into the chasm.

You and your men fall into the deep hole. Before you can try to get out, another crumbling building collapses on top of you. Bricks and wood crush you all. The last thing you hear is the terrifying cries of your horses.

THE END

To follow another path, turn to page 9.
To learn more about the earthquake, turn to page 103.

53

You listen to the horses' instincts and turn around, just as a giant chasm opens up in the street. Your heart leaps into your mouth. Thank goodness you changed direction!

But as you finally pull up to the hospital, you see that it's in ruins. Doctors and nurses hurry about, pushing patients into the streets in their beds or wheelchairs.

"Come on," you order your squad. "They need our help."

You ask a doctor where they want the patients to go, but he's flustered. "We set up an emergency hospital in the Mechanics Pavilion. Let's take them there."

You and your men load patients onto any wagons you can find. As you're about to move out, another fire engine pulls up. A fireman comes running up to you. His face is covered in soot.

"Forget Mechanics Pavilion. I've just come from there," he says. "It's caught fire."

"What happened?" you ask. You can't believe your bad luck.

"Someone in Hayes Valley was cooking ham and eggs in a broken chimney," the fireman says. "The fire got out of control. It spread fast up to City Hall and then Mechanics Pavilion. It's gone now . . . all gone."

"What do we do with these patients then?" you ask.

"A refugee camp is being set up in Golden Gate Park," another fireman says. "Maybe we can create a hospital there."

"Sounds like a plan," the doctor says.

To stay and help move patients, turn to page 56.
To transport patients to Golden Gate Park, turn to page 57.

You decide that you're going to stay and help get patients out of the hospital. You send your men ahead with patients on their wagons, and then you head into the ruined building.

As you're pushing an old man in a wheelchair toward the exit, you hear a loud noise.

CRACK!

You look up. A large beam from the ceiling comes crashing down on top of you. Just before it hits, you manage to push the old man out of the way. However, you are crushed under the beam's enormous weight.

When your squad hears of your death, they mourn you for days.

THE END

To follow another path, turn to page 9.
To learn more about the earthquake, turn to page 103.

Several military camps were set up around San Francisco. They provided shelter for the homeless as the city was rebuilt.

You decide to take the current patients to the park and make sure they're safe. When you get there, you see rows of tents. People are standing in long lines for food and water. Everything seems well organized. You marvel at how quickly things have been set up.

Soldiers help you set up several tents to create an emergency hospital. Soon, doctors and nurses are caring for many injured victims.

Turn the page.

As you head back to join your squad, you realize you haven't thought about your family.

Are my wife and baby safe? you wonder. You turn the horses in the direction of your home, but then another engine pulls up beside you.

"We have orders to report to the rail yard. We have to keep it from burning so the trains can run," the fireman says to you. "Pick up your squad, and head there immediately."

You worry about your family all the way back to the ruined hospital. *Surely, it would be okay to at least check in on them,* you think. As the rest of your squad climbs aboard the engine, you're torn.

To disobey orders and check on your family, turn to page 65.

To head to the rail yard, turn to page 68.

As you guide the horses toward First Street, you notice that many electrical power lines have snapped. They twist on the road like scared snakes, sparking tiny fires. Buildings on both sides of the street are crumbling. Broken brick, wood, and glass are scattered everywhere.

You can't move too quickly through the streets because of all the debris and rubble. You never thought you'd see your beautiful city crumble into dust like this.

"Fire!" someone shouts, and your training kicks in.

A few blocks away, a building is on fire. It's by a row of small apartment buildings. They're made mostly of wood. You know that if one of them catches fire, you could lose the entire row.

Turn the page.

You stop the horses at a safe distance and signal to the hose engine behind you to hook up to the fire hydrant. They work quickly, but nothing happens.

"Water! Hurry!" you call out.

But there's no water in the hydrant.

"The water mains must've burst," a fellow fireman says.

BOOM! An explosion in the distance tells you that the gas lines are bursting too. Another fire springs up on the other side of the street. The heat spreads quickly to envelop you.

"We must find water!" you cry.

To look for a working hydrant, go to page 61.
To evacuate the homes, turn to page 62.

There's no way to stop the fires without water. You spot a fire hydrant in the distance. Grabbing your wrench, you run toward it. All the way there, you pray that it has water. As you turn the cap of the hydrant, the warehouse in front of you bursts into flames.

The wall nearest you collapses. You're knocked out, and your legs are crushed under the rubble. When you wake, you find yourself in the hospital at Golden Gate Park. Your legs have been damaged beyond repair. The doctor recommends amputation.

You know this is the end of your career as a fireman. But when your wife and child appear at your bedside, you realize that you're just lucky to be alive.

THE END

To follow another path, turn to page 9.
To learn more about the earthquake, turn to page 103.

"We can't stop the fires . . . evacuate the homes!" You run into an apartment building and shout, "Everyone, get out!"

You help people escape as the fires spread quickly down the street. You've never seen anything like this.

When you walk into the backyard of one of the houses, you see that there are several families taking shelter there. You're glad to see them all safe. But then you spot someone cooking over an open fire in the corner of the yard.

"No cooking allowed," you say to the man of the house. "Put that fire out immediately. Everyone needs to leave. Now!" You realize you sound rude and frustrated. But it's more important to save lives than to be polite.

You head back to your engine. An engine from another fire station approaches.

"Our chief said a refugee camp is being set up at Golden Gate Park," the fireman says. "We're to inform all residents to head there or to the Ferry Building."

"What about these fires?" you ask.

"Without water, all we can do is let them burn," he says. "I've seen soldiers arriving. Maybe they'll do something."

"Let's hope so," you say, feeling helpless.

You and your squad spend the next few hours directing refugees to either the park or the docks. As you watch people dodging the dangers everywhere, you see a woman carrying a tiny baby. This makes you think about your own family.

You've been so busy that you haven't had time to even wonder about them. *Are they safe? Did they survive?*

Turn the page.

You want to go to them. You're tempted to run home and leave your fellow firemen so you can check on your family. But it would get you into big trouble.

Before you can make a decision, another engine arrives. The firemen on the wagon shout. "We've found a source of water! The Palace Hotel on Market. Let's go!"

Your squad hops onto your engine. They wait for you to make a move. You can barely move because your mind is on your own family. But all your fellow firefighters have families too.

Why should you be special? you ask yourself. If telephones were working, you could call, but they're not. You're filled with worry. Surely, your squad can spare you for a few hours.

To check on your family at home, go to page 65.

To head to the Palace Hotel, turn to page 72.

You order one of your squad members to take over driving the engine for you.

"I'll catch up to you soon. I want to make sure this neighborhood is safe." That's at least partly true. They don't know your home is only a few blocks away.

You run as fast as you can toward your apartment. You worry both about your family's safety and how much trouble you're going to be in. You might lose your job for this.

"I don't care," you say to yourself. "I have to make sure my family is safe."

The neighborhood where you live is completely engulfed in flames. You have to go a long way around to get to your street. You stop at one end and burst into tears.

Turn the page.

Fires sparked by the earthquake destroyed more than 20,000 buildings across the city.

The entire street of apartments is gone. All that's left are a few charred, blackened pillars.

"No, my family would've escaped," you say aloud. "They're survivors."

You hear a frightened whinny and follow the sound. Around the corner you find an abandoned horse and wagon.

You hop on and make your way through the debris. You see some neighbors looking through the mess that used to be their homes. You ask them if they've seen your wife and child. But no one has.

"Don't despair," an older man says to you. "Those who got away headed to Golden Gate Park."

You guide the horse back onto the road toward Golden Gate Park. You should've thought about looking for your family when you were there. You hear someone nearby shouting for help. You don't have time to stop. You have to find your family.

But what if they need you? you wonder. *What if it was your family that needed help, and no one stopped to help them?*

To stop and help, turn to page 75.
To keep going to the park, turn to page 77.

You say a quick prayer for your family's safety. Your squad members all have families too, and they must be as worried as you are. But you're firefighters, and today your city needs you.

On the way to the rail yard, you pass neighborhood after neighborhood on fire. Your heart sinks. It feels like an impossible mission. None of the hydrants are working, and water is nowhere to be found.

"The fire is spreading toward the rail yard!" one of your squad members shouts as you dodge a downed power line.

"Then we'd better hurry," you say, both to the men and to the horses. "If the rail yard burns, there's no way to get people out of the city."

The horses seem to understand the urgency. They pick up their pace, bravely facing their greatest fear—fire.

When you rush down another street near the waterfront, you see a sight that gives you hope. A Navy ship is hosing down a warehouse by pumping sea water from the bay. This works to put out the small fires that threaten these important buildings. Much of the city's goods are kept in these warehouses. It's vital that the docks are saved from the fire.

You all cheer the Navy ship as you drive past it to the rail yard. You get there just in time. The fire is across the street and threatens to jump over to the railway tracks.

Several engines arrive to help. They've been down to the docks to fill up on sea water and use that to put out nearby fires.

You and your fellow firemen spend the rest of the day and night filling the engines with sea water and pumping it onto the fires. It's hard work, but you barely notice how tired you are.

Turn the page.

By 2:30 a.m., the rail yard is safe. You're covered in sweat and soot. Your entire squad looks drained. The chief of your station arrives looking just as tired.

"Head to your families and get some rest," he says to all of you. "We're going to need you back on duty in a few hours."

You drive your fire engine back to the station. Your squad is silent. You know what they're thinking. None of you know where your families are. You've heard no word from them, and you're sure your neighborhoods have burned down.

"I'm just going to sleep at the station," you say out loud, as your heart sinks. "There isn't enough time for me to search for my family."

"Me, too," your men say one after the other.

When you pull into the station, you marvel that it's still standing. The fire must have missed it, and damage from the earthquake is minimal. Exhausted, you trudge up to the dorms.

There, in your bed, is your wife and baby—fast asleep. Your wife wakes up as you reach the bed.

"We didn't know where to go," she says. "And we didn't want you to worry about us. So we came here."

You're beyond happy. You hug your wife and baby and get some rest. In the morning, you'll be heading out again to put out more fires. But at least now you don't have to worry about your family's safety.

THE END

To follow another path, turn to page 9.
To learn more about the earthquake, turn to page 103.

You say a quick prayer for all the squad's families, and then head for the Palace Hotel. You guide your engine down Market Street. This street used to have the most magnificent buildings lining each side. Now, most of them look like charred skeletons. You remember passing the Palace Hotel on your way out earlier in the day. It made you happy to see that at least one building would survive the quake and fires.

But as you pull up to the hotel, you see that it, too, has suffered in the fires. Firemen are busy trying to put out the fire with their hoses. But before long, the hose they're carrying goes limp. They've used up all the water.

You frown and think hard. "What if we pump out the sewers? Would that help?" you ask one of the firemen

The fireman shrugs. "It can't hurt. Let's give it a try."

You and a few others access the sewers beneath the streets. Others run down the street to see if any other hydrants are working. Over the next few hours, you and your men do your best to try to save what you can. But with every little fire you put out, several more pop up. And pumping sewer water doesn't work. The pipes have burst, and the sewage just pours out onto the street.

Eventually, the terrible fires spread to the Palace Hotel.

Turn the page.

Finally, all you can do is stand back and watch as buildings are reduced to ash. Your heart sinks.

Soon, you and your men are ordered to help transport patients from the burning hospital to the emergency hospital at Golden Gate Park. You hear that many people who've lost their homes have also gone there. There's a chance that your family may be there as well.

You keep praying for their safety as you move patients to the park. After you've unloaded your third set of patients, you decide you can't wait any longer. You start looking for your family among the refugees.

Turn to page 77.

You decide you have to help. You pull into the street where a group of men are standing. On the ground is a lady covered in dirt. Her legs lie in an odd position. You know she needs medical attention.

"How can I help?" you ask one of the men.

The man looks relieved to see you. "We need to get her to the hospital."

You explain what's happened to the hospital building and how patients have been moved to the park. Then two soldiers appear, carrying two more bodies. They're very still.

"I'm afraid they're gone," a soldier says. You all shake your heads. There are going to be a lot more bodies to find before this is all over.

Turn the page.

You load the injured woman onto the wagon. The dead will be picked up later and taken to your fire station.

You feel bad about abandoning your fellow firefighters, but you think about your family. You're determined to find them.

You leave the man and the soldiers to keep looking for people as you steer the horse to the park. When you reach the emergency hospital, you help move the woman into a tent. You know she'll get help from the doctors there. You're glad to have saved a life. But now you need to find your wife and baby.

It takes you hours to search through the tents at Golden Gate Park. You ask everyone you meet, but they've not seen your family. While checking one more time at the hospital tent, you bump into your squad members. They're dropping off more patients.

An emergency hospital was set up at Golden Gate Park to treat those who were injured in the earthquake and fires.

Turn the page.

"Come on," they say. "Chief says we have to report back to the station."

You're hesitant to go, but your family is nowhere in sight. Finally, you agree to go with your squad.

When you arrive at the station, there's a huge surprise waiting for you. Your wife and child are waiting for you there!

"We wanted to let you know we were safe," your wife says. You hug them both, relieved that they're alive and well. You tell your wife to go to the refugee camp and promise to meet them there as soon as your shift is over.

As you watch them leave, your chief calls you over. "You disobeyed orders," he says. "You aren't the only one worried about family. After this is over, we'll have to review your promotion. I'm disappointed that you left your station."

You understand his anger and promise that you'll do your job to the best of your ability from now on. You owe your squad an apology, and you hope that they'll forgive you.

You spend the next two days working almost nonstop. When it begins to rain on Saturday, most of the fires are finally put out. Eventually you move your family out of San Francisco and head east. You'll never forget the terrible days when your city was reduced to rubble and ash.

THE END

To follow another path, turn to page 9.
To learn more about the earthquake, turn to page 103.

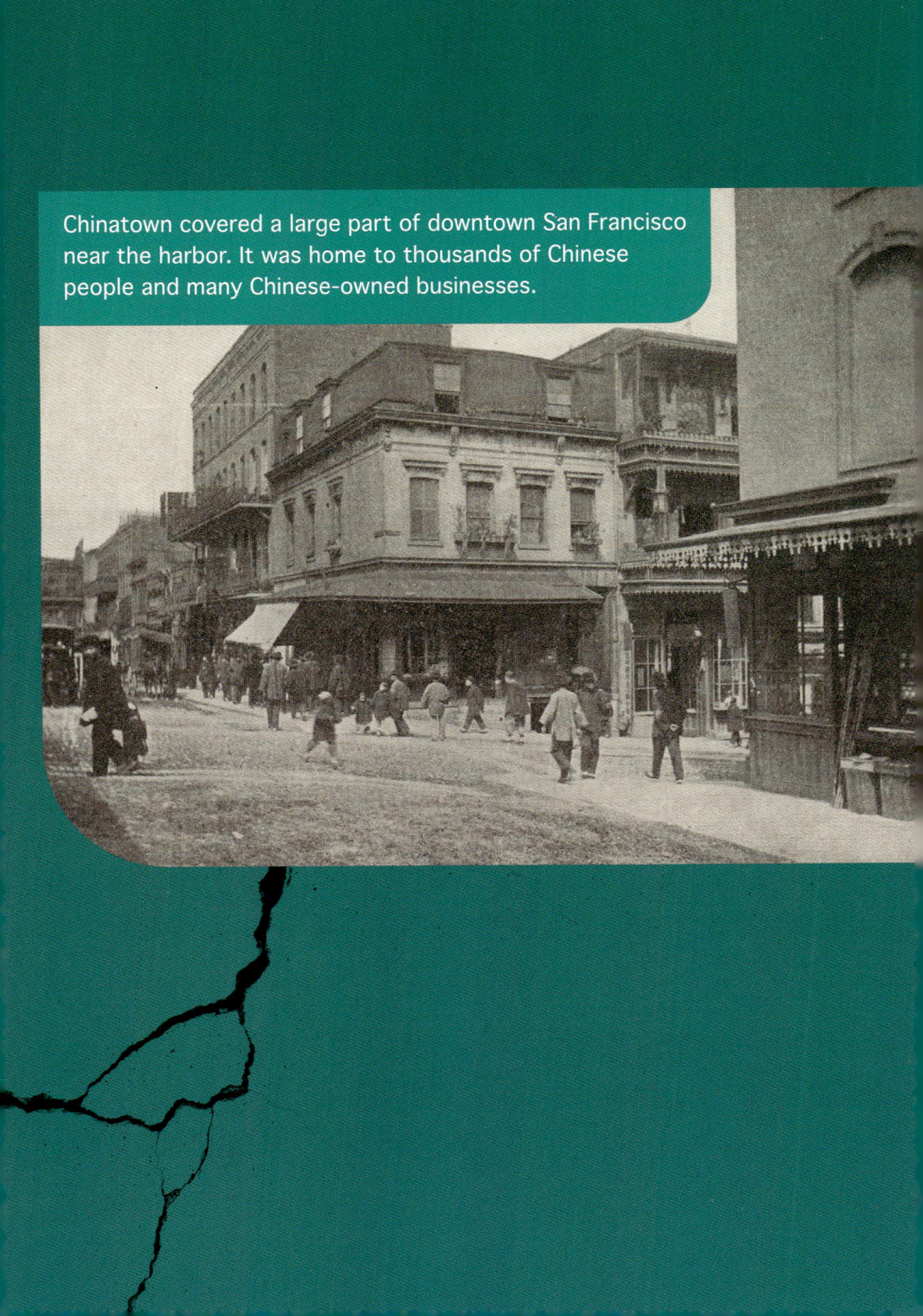

Chinatown covered a large part of downtown San Francisco near the harbor. It was home to thousands of Chinese people and many Chinese-owned businesses.

CHAPTER 4
CHINATOWN DISASTER

You run a small grocery shop in Chinatown. Your husband died a year ago. Since then, it's been hard to make enough money to raise your two sons. So you also work as a house cleaner to help make ends meet.

When you left home on April 18, 1906, you were expecting to be home again by about 8:00 a.m. You want to see your boys off to school before opening up the store for the day.

As you're wiping down the windows, the house begins to rumble and shake violently. A large beam in the ceiling cracks and falls right in the middle of the living room.

Turn the page.

You feel the floor roll under you like an ocean wave. Paintings and dishes fall and smash onto the floor. The window you were just cleaning shatters into a million pieces, spraying you with glass. You stumble to the doorway and hang on to the door jamb. You've heard that this is what you should do during an earthquake.

When the floor stops shaking, you look around. The house has been badly damaged. You begin to clean up the mess, but then another tremor hits. This time, you hide under the dining room table. You worry about your sons waking up to this horror all by themselves.

After the second tremor ends, you hear popping sounds. Then you smell smoke. When you crawl out from under the table, you notice that the next room is on fire.

> To try to save the house, go to page 83.
> To leave the house to burn, turn to page 85.

You can't bear to think of your employers losing their precious belongings. Their pet birds are shrieking in their cages. If nothing else, you should save them.

You run into the next room and see that the walls are already in flames. The two large bird cages swing violently as the birds panic and try to fly away. You can't reach high enough to unhook the cages from their hanging rod. So you decide to free the birds instead. You unlatch the doors, and the birds fly out. Unfortunately, one bird flies straight into the fire and dies immediately.

You run to the kitchen and pick up the nearest jug of water. You try to put out the fire, but it's no use. The fire is spreading too quickly. It's so hot you can feel your hair heating up. The second bird continues to fly around, looking for an escape. You open a large window just as the curtains catch fire.

Turn the page.

Thankfully, the bird escapes to safety. But the flames quickly rush up the fabric to the ceiling, and the burning curtains fall on you. They're heavy and drag you to the floor. Within moments, your clothes catch fire. You try to roll around to put out the flames, but you are quickly overcome.

Your family mourns your tragic death for many years.

THE END

To follow another path, turn to page 9.
To learn more about the earthquake, turn to page 103.

You see that the fire is spreading too quickly. There's no way to save anything. You have to run.

You head toward the door, but by now the curtains in the living room have caught fire. As you pass them, a piece of burning fabric falls onto your coat. You run through the door, panicking and screaming for help.

People stream out of their houses, but no one will stop to help you. The fire travels up the back of your coat. But as hard as you try, you can't get it off.

"Please! Help me!" you scream again.

A large man grabs you and tosses you to the ground. He rolls you over several times until your coat is no longer burning. It takes a moment for you to realize what's happened.

Turn the page.

"Thank you, sir," you say, gasping for air. "You saved my life."

The man's wife helps you up and offers you something to eat. You gobble the sandwich. You didn't realize you were so hungry.

You thank them over and over and introduce yourself. The woman tells you her name is Harriet and introduces her husband, William. Her children are John and Maisy.

The family asks you to join them as they seek refuge, but you have to get back to your children.

"I'm heading to Chinatown," you say, thinking of your boys all alone and scared. "Good luck, and stay safe."

You run, careful to avoid the giant cracks in the roads. You have to duck past burning buildings and the debris that lies everywhere.

You pass many people helping to dig victims out from under the rubble. You worry that your boys may be trapped somewhere too. So you pick up your pace.

As you approach Chinatown, you're relieved that the fires haven't reached this part of town. But there are obvious signs of damage from the quake. You rush down the street to your shop and your living quarters upstairs.

The shop looks like it survived the quake quite well. Only the front doors have fallen off their hinges and hang half open. You duck inside.

"Hey, stop!" You hear the voice of a man behind you. When you turn around, you're staring into the barrel of a gun. "Come out of the store, slowly," the man says.

Turn the page.

Your legs feel weak as you step outside again. When you can focus on the man, you see that he's a policeman.

"The mayor says no looting is allowed," the policeman says. His voice quivers. "I'm supposed to shoot on sight."

"This is muh-muh-my shop," you stammer.

"Can you prove it?" he asks. "You'd better come with me to the police station."

You can't leave without knowing if your boys are safe. But you know the policeman will not ask you again.

> To plead with the officer, go to page 89.
> To go with the policeman, turn to page 92.

You begin to cry. "Please don't shoot me. My children are upstairs. I need to know if they're safe."

The policeman's gun wavers, and you can't take your eyes off it.

"You could be lying," he says. "If I let you go, you might steal everything in this store."

You blink away the tears. There must be something you can say to convince him. Just then, you hear the soft padding of feet climbing down the stairs.

"Mama!" A scared child calls from inside the shop. Out of the shop come two little boys. They wrap their arms around your waist and cry when they see the gun pointed at you. You hush them without moving too much.

"See, officer," you say. "These are my sons. They live here. We . . . live here."

Turn the page.

The policeman exhales and lowers his gun. "That was a close call," he says, putting his gun away. "You really should be more careful."

You're shaking in fear, but you offer him some food to take with him. He accepts gratefully and disappears down the street.

"We were so scared," your sons tell you. They share how they were thrown from their beds when the quake hit. They called out for you, but you weren't there.

You hug your sons closely. "The city is on fire," you say. "We should leave."

Quickly, you pack a few things and head out the door. As you leave, your neighbors walk by.

"We're going to stay here and protect our town," they say. "We'll make a line of buckets and put out any fires that come our way. You should stay with us."

> The fires that destroyed many of the buildings on Market Street quickly spread to Chinatown nearby.

You saw the terrible fires near Market Street. If that spreads to Chinatown, there's no way you can save your buildings. But perhaps the fires won't come this way.

To stay and fight the fires, turn to page 94.
To leave and look for safety, turn to page 99.

The policeman takes you to the nearest station. The entire time you are sobbing and begging him to believe you.

"My sons are in that building," you cry. "I don't even know if they're safe."

The policeman is unconcerned. He marches you to the station. When you arrive, you notice that the windows have no glass in them. Some of the roof has fallen onto the street. Still, the policeman pushes you inside and makes you sit at a table. He fires several questions at you, which you answer in between sobs.

"We've been ordered to evacuate," another policeman stops and says to you both.

"What do we do with prisoners?" the first officer asks.

"I'm not a prisoner," you say, wiping your eyes. "That was my shop."

The second officer looks at you. "You're Mrs. Lee, from the grocery store in Chinatown, right?"

What a relief to be recognized! The second officer confirms that you're telling the truth. You run home to find your boys waiting for you inside.

"Let's leave quickly," you say as you hug them tight. "It's not safe. The fires are on their way here."

You all pack your things and head out. As you leave your shop, your neighbors walk by. "We're staying to protect our town," they say. "We'll carry water in buckets to put out any fires. You should stay and help."

You saw the huge fires near Market Street. If they spread to Chinatown, there will be no way to save anything.

To stay and help your neighbors, turn to page 94.
To take your sons to safety, turn to page 99.

For the rest of the day, you and your boys clean up the mess in the shop. You hear explosions throughout the day. At first they were in the distance, but they seem to get closer by the hour. You and the boys spend the night huddled in the storeroom. Early the next morning, you wake to the sound of shouting outside.

You go to see what's happening and see that the neighbors have formed a line. Just beyond the entrance to Chinatown, the city is ablaze. The fires are headed your way! You grab several buckets and fill them with water. Then you take your place in line with your neighbors.

It doesn't take long for the fire to spread into Chinatown. The first building falls quickly. Because everything is built so close together, the flames easily jump from building to building. All the water in the buckets barely reduces the fire.

"We have to run," you shout to your neighbors.

You go and get your sons. Picking up your bags, you lead the boys through the store. But the door has already caught fire. Tongues of fire lick the ceiling, consuming the beams within seconds. The baskets of fruit and food burst into flame.

Your boys cling to you as you seek a way out. The front of the store is a wall of fire. You turn to the back door, but a beam from the ceiling falls and blocks your path.

To run out the front door, turn to page 96.
To run out the back door, turn to page 97.

There's a gap in the fire that leads out the front door. You believe you can make it if you run through fast. There's no time to think. It's now or never.

"Come on," you say to the boys. Gripping their hands, you make a dash for the exit.

But as you cross the threshold, the beam holding up the door collapses. You and the boys are crushed. The firemen don't find your bodies until the fires have all been put out. Your neighbors mourn the loss of you and your boys for a long time.

THE END

To follow another path, turn to page 9.
To learn more about the earthquake, turn to page 103.

You look for a way to get over the beam, but it's impossible. The fire has completely engulfed the doorway. It's too late to head to the front door too. So, in a panic, you run back into the storeroom.

You hold your boys close and pray for a miracle. The room fills with smoke, and it becomes hard to breathe. You pass out, holding your children.

When you wake up, you're lying on a narrow hospital bed inside a large tent.

"Where are my boys?" you croak.

"They're safe, dear," a nurse tells you. "You're at the emergency hospital in Golden Gate Park."

Turn the page.

Your sons are nearby sharing a sandwich. They seem to be fine. You got your miracle. Although you lost your home and shop, you have your children.

Two days later, you leave the hospital on Saturday. It's raining, and the fires have gone out. Sadly, Chinatown has been destroyed, along with your shop and home. But soon you and your neighbors get together and begin to rebuild. You help each other, and you know that someday, you'll have a home again.

THE END

To follow another path, turn to page 9.
To learn more about the earthquake, turn to page 103.

You feel bad for abandoning your neighbors, but your boys' safety comes first. Ducking past several fires, you dash around large cracks in the roads and avoid the broken electric cables.

You turn toward Golden Gate Park, but the streets have been blocked. Soldiers are redirecting people away from certain streets.

"What's going on?" you ask a soldier.

"We're going to set explosives here," he says. "The only way to stop the fires from spreading is to blow up some buildings in their path. The fires should then burn themselves out."

That plan doesn't make sense to you. But you hope they know what they're doing. People seem to be heading to the docks, so you join them. As you get closer, you see boats spraying the buildings with sea water. If only Chinatown was closer, maybe your home could be saved.

Turn the page.

Eventually, you reach the Ferry Building. It's tilted but still standing. Fireboats are frantically spraying water onto the Ferry Building.

You join the long line of people waiting to board a ferry. The line moves slowly, and it's almost the next morning when you reach the front of it.

You get on a ferry, and it takes you to the other side of the bay. You have no money and don't know anyone on this side. But you're led to a park where volunteers give you a tent for the night. They also give out clothes and food.

You stay there for the next three days. When the rain falls on Saturday, you hear that the fires are finally put out. You stay for a few more days and then head back to Chinatown.

You don't recognize your neighborhood. Everything has been burned down. But your neighbors are there.

Like much of the rest of San Francisco, little was left of Chinatown after the fires went out.

You help to set up tents for people to sleep in. Everyone promises to help each other rebuild. The boys find a way to play with their friends among the ruins. Slowly, you help bring Chinatown back to life.

THE END

To follow another path, turn to page 9.
To learn more about the earthquake, turn to page 103.

The ruins of City Hall after the Great San Francisco Earthquake and fires of 1906

CHAPTER 5
AFTERMATH

The stories in this book are based on the experiences of real people who survived the Great San Francisco Earthquake in 1906. You can read some of their stories on the website of the Museum of the City of San Francisco.

For many young people who experienced this quake, the horror was not easily forgotten. For a long time, one person had nightmares about being swallowed by the earth. Others became afraid to be left alone or feared lightning and thunder for the rest of their lives.

One man who sold musical instruments and phonographs watched as his store burned. He saved some of his precious books and stored them in a friend's building.

However, the next day he discovered that his friend's store had burned down too. Like many others, he lost everything. After the quake, he began selling real estate instead.

Famed photographer Ansel Adams was just four years old when the quake happened. The tremor slammed him into a wall, and he broke his nose. It never healed properly. Friends often teased him about it, calling it his "earthquake nose."

Many firefighters and soldiers were killed in their attempts to save the city and its people. Many who survived also acted bravely trying to put out fires or help move people to safety.

The 1906 San Francisco earthquake was one of the worst natural disasters in history. About 3,000 people were killed in the quake and the resulting fires. By the end of that fateful week, 225,000 of the city's 400,000 residents were homeless.

The disaster was incredibly costly. Almost 28,000 buildings across 500 city blocks were destroyed. The fires burned more than 4.7 square miles (12.2 square kilometers.) The damage cost at least $400 million, which would be more than $11 billion in today's money.

The Great San Francisco Earthquake was one of the biggest and costliest disasters in U.S. history.

MORE ABOUT EARTHQUAKES

Today, we measure earthquakes on the Richter scale. The scale didn't exist in 1906, but scientists think the Great San Francisco Earthquake would have measured 8.3 on the Richter scale. It was caused by movement on the San Andreas fault line. Scientists think that the tectonic plates there shifted more than 20 feet (6.1 meters)!

Since the 1906 quake, there have been several powerful and historic earthquakes around the world:

- The 1960 Valdivia Earthquake in Chile, South America, is the most powerful earthquake ever recorded. It measured 9.5 on the Richter scale. Thousands were killed or injured, and at least 2 million people were left homeless.

- In 1964, a 9.2 magnitude quake in Alaska left 131 people dead.

- In 2004, a 9.2 quake near the island of Sumatra and the resulting tsunami left more than 225,000 people dead across several countries. The quake lasted nearly 10 minutes, which is the longest earthquake ever recorded.

EARTHQUAKE MAGNITUDE SCALE

Description	Magnitude
Usually not felt, but can be recorded by topography	1.0-1.9
	2.0-2.9
Vibrations detected	3.0-3.9
	4.0-4.9
Windows rattle or break; light damage	5.0-5.9
Cracks in buildings; falling branches	6.0-6.9
	7.0-7.9
Buildings collapse; landslides	8.0-8.9
Devastation; many deaths	9.0 and greater

OTHER PATHS TO EXPLORE

>>> Imagine you're living in San Francisco when the earthquake struck in 1906. If you were shaken from your sleep, what would be your first reaction? Knowing what we do today about earthquakes, what would you do differently?

>>> Firefighters are everyday heroes, but on that fateful day, their job was made much harder because water was hard to find. If you were a firefighter in San Francisco after the earthquake, where would you look for water? What other ways would you try to put out the fires?

>>> Imagine you're a newspaper journalist living through the earthquake and fires. The telephones and telegraphs aren't working. You know it's important to get the news out to people around the country and the world. They might be able to help. What would you write? Which stories would you find the most compelling to write about? And how would you make sure the story was shared in other cities?

BIBLIOGRAPHY

Chippendale, Lisa A. *The San Francisco Earthquake of 1906.* Philadelphia: Chelsea House Publishers, 2001.

Tarshis, Lauren. *I Survived the San Francisco Earthquake, 1906.* New York: Scholastic Inc., 2012.

Smith, Dennis. *San Francisco Is Burning: The Untold Story of the 1906 Earthquake and Fires.* New York: Viking, 2005.

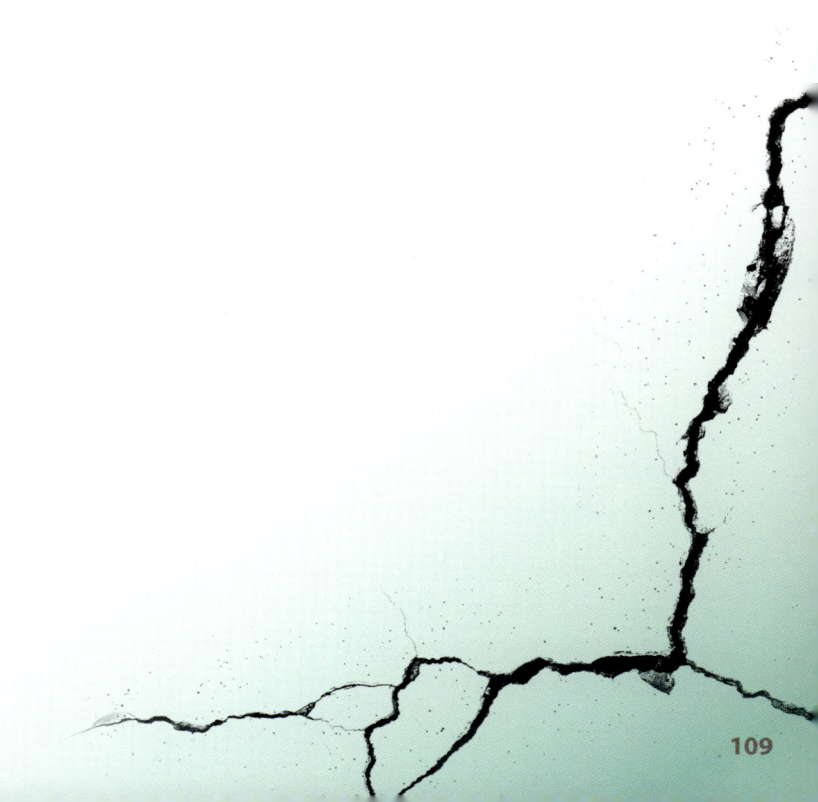

GLOSSARY

amputation (am-pyuh-TAY-shun)—the removal of an arm or a leg because it is badly damaged

chasm (KAZ-uhm)—a long, wide crack or gorge in Earth's surface

donation (doh-NAY-shuhn)—a gift or contribution, usually for charity

evacuate (i-VA-kyuh-wayt)—to leave an area during a time of danger

fault (FAWLT)—a crack in Earth's crust where two plates meet; earthquakes often occur along faults

jamb (JAM)—the vertical sides of a doorway, window, or other opening

magnitude (MAG-nuh-tood)—a measure of the amount of energy released by an earthquake

refugee camp (reh-fyuh-JEE KAMP)—a place where people who were forced to leave their homes can receive shelter, food, and water

salvage (SAL-vij)—to save property from being destroyed or thrown out

tectonic plate (tek-TAH-nik PLAYT)—a giant slab of Earth's crust that moves around on magma; the movement of tectonic plates can create volcanoes and cause earthquakes

READ MORE

Bybee, Veeda. *Lily and the Great Quake: A San Francisco Earthquake Survival Story*. North Mankato, MN: Stone Arch Books, 2020.

Loh-Hagan, Virginia. *When the Ground Shook: San Francisco Earthquake of 1906*. Ann Arbor, MI: Cherry Lake Publishing, 2020.

Romero, Libby. *All About Earthquakes*. New York: Children's Press, 2021.

INTERNET SITES

San Francisco Before and After the 1906 Earthquake
openculture.com/2018/05/see-footage-of-san-francisco-right-before-after-the-massively-devastating-earthquake-of-1906.html

The San Francisco Earthquake
pbs.org/wgbh/americanexperience/features/ansel-san-francisco-earthquake/

What to Do Before, During, or After an Earthquake
lifesecure.com/earthquake-safety-tips-earthquake/

ABOUT THE AUTHOR

Photo by:
Pierre Folrev, Folrev Photography

Ailynn Collins is the author of several books for kids, from stories about space and aliens, to You Choose stories and nonfiction books. She has a master's degree in writing for children and young adults from Hamline University. She's lived all over the world and speaks six languages. When she's not writing, she's competing in dog sports with one of her five dogs, or showing them in dog shows.

Photo Credits
Alamy: Antiqua Print Gallery, 80, Better Late Images, 40, ClassicStock, 48, Everett Collection Historical, 57, Everett Collection Inc, 34, Science History Images, 91, Universal Images Group North America LLC, 101, UPI, 105; Getty Images: Sepia Times, 6; Library of Congress Prints and Photographs Division, Cover, 15, 66, A. Blumberg, 22, C.L. Wasson., 29, H.C. White Co., 27, 52, Pillsbury Picture Co., 77; Shutterstock: Everett Collection, 10, 73, 102, komkrit Preechachanwate, design element , Cover, trgrowth, 107